# Ferdinand Magellan

Elaine Landau

LERNER PUBLICATIONS COMPANY • MINNEAPOLIS

Illustrations by Tim Parlin

Lerner Publications Company
A division of Lerner Publishing Group
241 First Avenue North
Minneapolis, MN 55401 U.S.A.

Website address: www.lernerbooks.com

Library of Congress Cataloging-in-Publication Data

Landau, Elaine.
    Ferdinand Magellan / by Elaine Landau.
        p.    cm. — (History maker bios)
    Includes bibliographical references and index.
    ISBN-13: 978-0-8225-2942-4 (lib. bdg. : alk. paper)
    ISBN-10: 0-8225-2942-4 (lib. bdg. : alk. paper)
    1. Magalhães, Fernão de, d. 1521—Juvenile literature.  2. Explorers—Portugal—Biography—Juvenile literature.  3. Voyages around the world—Juvenile literature.  I. Title.  II. Series.
    G286.M2L36  2005
    910'.92—dc22                                                      2004028888

Manufactured in the United States of America
1  2  3  4  5  6 – JR – 10  09  08  07  06  05

# TABLE OF CONTENTS

INTRODUCTION                          5

1. AT THE START                       6

2. SERVING HIS HOMELAND              11

3. ONWARD TO SPAIN!                  16

4. ON THE SEA                        21

5. MAGELLAN'S LAST DAYS              32

TIMELINE                             44
DEAD RECKONING                       45
FURTHER READING                      46
WEBSITES                             47
SELECT BIBLIOGRAPHY                  47
INDEX                                48

# INTRODUCTION

In modern times, maps show every part of the world. But five hundred years ago, no one was sure where one ocean ended and another began or where all the continents were. Many Europeans believed Earth was flat. Over time, explorers helped change this view of the world.

Ferdinand Magellan was one of these daring explorers. He led the first voyage around the world. His expedition showed that Earth is twice as big as people had believed. And the journey proved that the world is round. Ferdinand faced great danger during his travels. But he refused to give up.

This is his story.

# 1 AT THE START

Ferdinand Magellan was born about 1480 in Portugal, a country in western Europe. Ferdinand was the youngest of three children. He had a brother named Diogo and a sister named Isabel.

The Magellans were related to Portugal's royalty. They ran a large farm in northwest Portugal. The family's land sat among mountains, not far from the seacoast.

Ferdinand started school when he was seven years old. He studied reading, writing, math, and a language called Latin. After school each day, he helped his parents grow wheat and rye on their farm. He also helped care for the sheep, goats, and pigs.

When he was about twelve years old, Ferdinand became a royal page. He served Queen Leonora at the palace in Lisbon, Portugal's capital. Ferdinand carried messages, ran errands, and did chores at the palace.

*King John II and Queen Leonora of Portugal kneel in prayer in this drawing printed in 1495.*

Ferdinand also continued his schooling. He studied art, math, music, and history. He learned to use a sword and to dance. Like most Europeans of that time, Ferdinand was Christian. Studying religion and keeping his faith was important to him. Ferdinand's favorite subject, however, was navigation. He liked to study maps. He wanted to learn all about sailing ships and exploring the world by sea.

## COLUMBUS COMES TO LISBON

In 1493, Christopher Columbus returned from the Americas. His ships found shelter from a storm in Lisbon. His arrival caused a great stir, and young Ferdinand was swept up in the excitement. Columbus had met natives in the Americas. Europeans didn't even know that people lived on the other side of the world.

Ferdinand lived during the Age of Discovery. Beginning in the mid-1400s, European explorers set out in search of new sea trading routes. Kings and merchants were especially eager for faster routes to the Spice Islands. Europeans gave this name to the Molucca Islands in southeastern Asia. This region is rich in spices such as pepper, cinnamon, ginger, and cloves. Europeans highly valued spices. They used them to preserve meat and to make bland food more flavorful.

Columbus sailed to find sea routes and to claim land for Spain.

Lisbon was a major seaport and an exciting city for Ferdinand. He watched ships dock and unload their goods from far-off places. He saw explorers return from their adventures. Some arrived with gold, silk, gems, and other riches.

Portugal's king, John II, encouraged explorers. He believed they would make Portugal great. Successful explorers became rich and famous. They were heroes, and everyone looked up to them. Ferdinand dreamed of being an explorer and sailing the seas.

# 2 SERVING HIS HOMELAND

**F**erdinand stayed in Lisbon after finishing his service as a page. He became a clerk at a government office called India House. Ferdinand and other workers kept records of Portugal's sea trade and exploration. There, he studied maps and read reports from explorers. He learned about preparing ships for long voyages.

Ferdinand's chance to go to sea finally came in 1505. By this time, Portugal was a leading sea power. The new king, Manuel I, wanted even greater glory for his country. He launched a major expedition. Fleets of ships carrying soldiers and weapons set sail for Africa and India. Their goal was to capture important seaports and take control of trading routes to Asia.

Ferdinand signed up for service. He hoped to win the respect of King Manuel I by fighting for Portugal. The king did not like Ferdinand, probably because the Magellan family had not supported Manuel's claim to the throne after King John II died.

*King Manuel I of Portugal lived from 1469 to 1521. He became king in 1495.*

## SAILING SHIPS

In Magellan's time, full-rigged ships were the most common ships to sail the seas. This type of ship had three tall poles called masts. A mainmast stood in the middle of the ship, a foremast was in the front, and a mizzenmast was in the back. Each mast held one big square sail and one smaller square sail. Weapons, food, and supplies were stored below deck. Only the captain and some officers had cabins. The crew slept on the deck or in hammocks below deck.

Ferdinand was on one of twenty-two Portuguese ships bound for India. The Portuguese were fierce fighters. They sank enemy fleets and captured cities. Ferdinand fought hard and was wounded several times in battle. He also saved many of his fellow sailors.

The commander praised Ferdinand's bravery and called him a good leader. Before long, he became an assistant captain. He sharpened his military skills. And he learned to run a ship and properly chart a ship's course. Then in 1513, Ferdinand received a serious wound in battle. An enemy's spear went through his leg. Ferdinand would walk with a limp for the rest of his life.

Captain General Francisco de Almeida was the commander for Ferdinand's first ocean voyage.

Ferdinand returned to Lisbon. He had served his country well for eight years. He hoped to be honored and respected. But King Manuel I had not changed his mind about Ferdinand. He even refused to give Ferdinand a small increase in his military pay.

Ferdinand worked hard to gain favor with the king. He wanted to set up a base in the Spice Islands. Ferdinand knew it would bring great riches to Portugal. But the king would not provide money for the voyage.

Ferdinand saw that there was no future for him in Portugal. He asked King Manuel I for permission to serve another country. The king didn't care about Ferdinand. He told him to do as he wished. So Ferdinand set off for Spain, Portugal's rival in the sea trade. Ferdinand hoped for a brighter future in Spain.

# 3 ONWARD TO SPAIN!

**F**erdinand arrived in the Spanish city of Seville in the fall of 1517. He came with high hopes and big dreams. Ferdinand had spent the past months in Portugal studying maps and charts. He had talked with many explorers and ships' pilots about navigating the seas. Mathematicians and scientists taught him about charting a ship's location.

Soon Ferdinand developed some interesting ideas of his own. At that time, European trading ships sailed east to reach the Spice Islands. But Ferdinand was eager to try a different route. He hoped to get there by sailing west.

Ferdinand had heard about a waterway through South America. This passage connected the Atlantic Ocean to another ocean off the continent's west coast. He didn't know how wide this other sea was. No European had sailed across it. But Ferdinand figured it couldn't be too far to the Spice Islands from South America.

*In this drawing from the late 1500s, Ferdinand is using navigation tools to plan his route to the Spice Islands.*

Ferdinand hoped Spain's young king, Charles I, would sponsor his voyage to the Spice Islands. It took months, but Ferdinand's plan finally sparked the interest of an official. He arranged a meeting with the king.

Ferdinand impressed King Charles I. Ferdinand appeared strong and confident as he presented his plan. He spoke plainly and clearly. Ferdinand believed his voyage would change maps of the world. The Spice Islands might be only a day's journey west of South America. It was possible that Spain could lay claim to them. The idea excited King Charles I. He put his full support behind Ferdinand's plan. He would pay for the entire voyage.

Spain's King Charles I liked Ferdinand's plan to sail west to the Spice Islands. King Charles I was seventeen years old at that time.

*When Ferdinand was a boy, European maps of the world did not show North and South America. Ferdinand's voyage would change maps.*

Not everyone was excited about Ferdinand's plans. A powerful businessman named Cristóbal de Haro had offered to pay for the trip. He wanted a share of the expedition's riches. It angered him to be pushed aside. One of the king's advisers, Juan de Fonseca, felt strongly that a Spaniard should lead the voyage. These two men plotted against Ferdinand. Fonseca hired three of the expedition's captains. Haro urged these men to rebel against Ferdinand at sea.

It's a wonder that Ferdinand ever set sail. So many people were working against him. Yet on September 20, 1519, he did just that.

Ferdinand had five ships in his command: *Trinidad, San Antonio, Concepción, Victoria,* and *Santiago.* Crowds cheered as the ships left the harbor. Ferdinand was finally living his dream. He was an explorer sailing for the Americas and the unknown.

## SUPPLIES FOR SURVIVAL

Ferdinand made a supply list for the journey. The ships would carry a limited supply of food. They included olive oil, dried codfish, salted pork, sardines, cheese, wine, and water. Nearly as important as food were trinkets. Ferdinand hoped the natives the sailors met would give them food. In exchange, the crew could trade small bells, beads, mirrors, and combs. Ferdinand also brought lances, spears, crossbows, and other weapons. And he gathered navigational tools to help chart their course.

# 4 ON THE SEA

**F**erdinand was a strict but able commander to his crew of 277 men. Most of the sailors came from Spain or Portugal. Others came from France, Germany, Italy, Greece, and Africa.

Ferdinand set rules for everyone to follow. Every man would receive a limited amount of food each day. And the whole crew would take part in daily prayers. Ferdinand held strong Christian beliefs and wanted others to share his faith.

The first stop on the voyage was the Canary Islands off the west coast of Africa. The ships took on extra wood, water, vegetables, and other supplies. Ferdinand also received a message sent by fast ship. It warned him that the captains chosen by Fonseca would try to rebel.

*Many seafarers, including Columbus and Magellan, stopped at the Canary Islands for supplies.*

The fleet then set sail for South America. Ferdinand took quick action when one of the captains refused to follow the course he had chosen. Ferdinand locked him up and made an example of him.

At first, the weather was pleasant. Wind filled the sails and pushed the fleet southwest. But the sea turned stormy about two weeks later. Rough waves tossed the ships. The men were frightened. Some felt doomed. Many fell to their knees crying and praying.

In Magellan's time, strong winds could make sea travel dangerous—as shown in this painting from the mid-1500s.

Wind fills the sails of Ferdinand's ship, the VICTORIA.

Finally, the storms passed. But the crew's troubles weren't over. Next, they sailed into a hot, nearly breezeless area called the doldrums. The ships drifted under the hot sun for weeks. The heat felt unbearable. Men fainted. Much of their food spoiled. Sharks circled the ships. The crew wondered how much longer they could stand it. Then a light wind fluttered in the sails. The ships began to move with some speed again.

On November 20, 1519, Ferdinand's small fleet crossed the equator. This imaginary line around Earth divides the world into northern and southern halves. The ships sailed into the southern half. Soon the fleet neared Brazil on the east coast of South America. Ferdinand directed the ships into a harbor. White beaches and tree-covered mountains lined the deep blue water. The crew dropped anchor near what would become the city of Rio de Janeiro.

*Other explorers arrived in South America before Magellan. Pedro Álvares Cabral claimed Brazil for the king of Portugal in 1500.*

Ferdinand had chosen a good place to stop. It was summer in South America, and the weather was warm. The natives in that part of Brazil were friendly. Sailors offered them trinkets. In return, the men had their fill of pineapples, sweet potatoes, roast pig, and chicken. The crew stayed in Brazil for a few weeks. They repaired their ships and took on new supplies.

## A CHANGE OF SEASONS

An imaginary line called the equator divides the world into northern and southern halves. The northern half and the southern half have opposite seasons. When it's summer in the North, it's winter in the South. Europe is in the northern half of the world. Ferdinand and his crew crossed the equator on their way to South America. They had to get used to summer in December and winter in July.

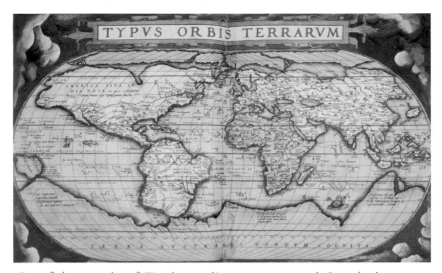

*Careful records of Ferdinand's route around South America added many details to future maps of the world. This map was published in 1570.*

The fleet continued sailing down the east coast of South America. Ferdinand explored the bays, rivers, and inlets they passed. He was sure they would find the passage across the continent soon. But the weather grew colder, and strong winds began to blow. The fleet was sailing south toward the frozen continent of Antarctica. As the days passed, traveling became more difficult. The men on deck shivered in the cold. Their wet clothes turned icy on their bodies. The food supply was low, and everyone felt hunger pangs.

The fleet stayed close to the rocky shoreline and kept searching for the passage. The ships came to a few small islands. Crewmembers were amazed at the strange animals they saw. Creatures they called "black geese" were penguins. "Sea wolves" were actually sea lions. The men had never seen animals like these before. They killed and ate some of the animals. The meat kept their stomachs full for a while.

Ferdinand's black geese were later named Magellanic penguins in his honor.

But soon many of the men were feeling desperate. Some begged Ferdinand to return to Brazil or go back to Spain. Others wanted to turn around and take the eastern route to the Spice Islands. Ferdinand refused to listen to them. He pushed on, sure that the passage was just ahead.

The weather grew even colder. Storms battered the ships. Relief didn't come for several weeks. At the end of March 1520, the fleet made anchor at Port San Julian on the coast of modern-day Argentina. The crew rested, repaired their ships, and gathered supplies.

*Port San Julian was named for Saint Julian (BELOW RIGHT). In Roman Catholicism, he is a patron saint of travelers and sailors.*

Shortly after arriving, the rebellious captains sprang into action again. They spoke against Ferdinand to their shipmates. They urged the others to join them in taking over the expedition. This time, the rebels nearly succeeded. But after a bloody fight, Ferdinand and his supporters managed to regain control.

*Ships like Ferdinand's carried cannons, swords, and guns called muskets. The weapons were for battle. But sometimes sailors used these weapons to fight each other.*

Ferdinand would not give up. He was determined to find the western route to the Spice Islands. He had to get there. He would not return to Spain defeated.

Ferdinand tried to use his time in San Julian wisely. After the crew repaired the *Santiago*, he sent it to search for the passage. The crew wasn't successful. But they did find a harbor that they named Santa Cruz. This place offered better shelter from the cold and more animals to hunt.

On the way back to San Julian, however, the worst happened. A strong storm tore away the ship's sails. The *Santiago* barely made it to shore. Then waves destroyed the ship. All but one of the crew survived. Ferdinand had lost a ship. And he still had not found the passage.

# 5 MAGELLAN'S LAST DAYS

**B**y October 1520, the weather was growing warmer. Ferdinand's smaller fleet set sail from Santa Cruz. He prayed that the passage was near. Three days later, his prayers were answered. On October 21, the ships entered the waterway Ferdinand had longed to find.

Two ships went ahead to explore the passage and returned with joyful news. The men were certain another ocean lay at the end of the waterway.

The passage would later be called the Strait of Magellan. But the strait was not what Ferdinand had imagined. It lay between the tip of South America and a group of steep, rocky islands. The waterway often twisted and narrowed. Icy cliff walls dropped straight to the sea. The crew fought strong currents and winds. It was a dangerous path, not a quick route to another ocean.

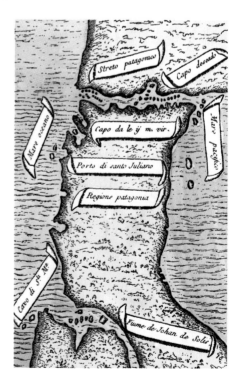

*Antonio Pigafetta, an Italian on Ferdinand's voyage, drew this map of the Strait of Magellan. Unlike modern maps, NORTH is at the bottom of Pigafetta's map.*

Soon Ferdinand had other worries. The captain of the *San Antonio* bolted partway through the passage. He turned his ship around and headed back to Spain. It was a terrible loss. The *San Antonio* was carrying nearly all the food.

Ferdinand's three remaining ships exited the strait in the last week of November. The journey through the passage had taken thirty-eight days. The strait stretched 334 miles. But at last, the fleet floated in calm waters. Ferdinand saw a great sea shining under sunny skies. He named the ocean Mar Pacífico, meaning "peaceful sea." In English, it is called the Pacific Ocean.

Magellan expected to reach the Spice Islands within days. Instead, several weeks passed with no sign of land. The men were scared. The Pacific Ocean proved to be much larger than anyone had ever dreamed. Food and supplies soon ran low, and the men began to starve. Some of the sailors caught and ate the ships' rats. But soon even these creatures were gone. The crew started eating sawdust and chewing on bits of leather. If their luck didn't change soon, the entire crew would die at sea.

*Ferdinand and his crew were unprepared to sail across the vast Pacific Ocean.*

The fleet had been sailing the Pacific for more than three months. A lookout finally spotted an island on March 6, 1521. The crew thought they'd be saved. But soon their relief turned to fear. The island's natives paddled toward them in canoes. The natives boarded the *Trinidad* and grabbed whatever they could carry. Before leaving, they cut loose the longboat tied to the ship. Magellan was angry. The fleet needed the longboat. It could dock where a larger ship could not. Without it, there would be places the fleet couldn't stop for food.

Ships' crews used small, light longboats (BELOW LEFT) to travel across shallow waters.

*Ferdinand and his crew sailed the Pacific Ocean for three months before they sighted this beautiful island. They had to battle the islanders to get food and supplies. In modern times, the island is known as Guam.*

Ferdinand led a band of men ashore. The crew killed several natives and burned dozens of huts and boats. Ferdinand found the longboat. He and his men filled it with the natives' food and took it back to his ships. Ferdinand was not proud of his actions. But he put it behind him and sailed on. He named that island the Isle of Thieves. In modern times, it is known as Guam.

About ten days later, the crew spotted other islands. They anchored their ships, and Ferdinand claimed the land for Spain. These islands would later be called the Philippines. Ferdinand had only one wish. He hoped the natives would welcome them.

At first, the natives were kind and helpful. They gave Ferdinand and his men fruit, meat, and water. In return, Ferdinand gave them small mirrors and other shiny trinkets.

*Some islanders welcomed Ferdinand and his men. In modern times, these islands are called the Philippines.*

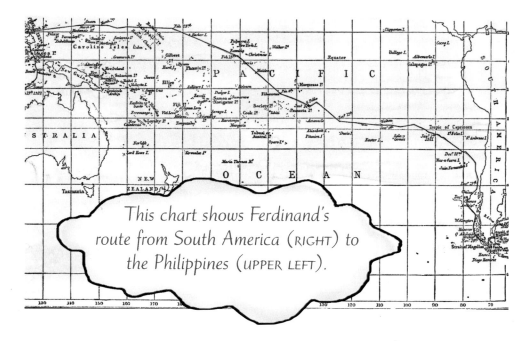

This chart shows Ferdinand's route from South America (RIGHT) to the Philippines (UPPER LEFT).

About a week later, Ferdinand visited another island in the Philippines called Cebu. The island's leader was named Humabon. He and his people welcomed the men too.

A Catholic priest sailed with Ferdinand. The priest told the islanders about Christianity. Many natives decided to become Christians. On April 15, 1521, the priest baptized more than five hundred people during Easter services. Ferdinand felt overjoyed. His faith remained strong, and he believed spreading Christianity was his duty.

But then he tried to bring Christianity to Humabon's enemies. They lived on the nearby island of Mactan. Humabon warned Ferdinand about the natives of Mactan. Ferdinand didn't care about the risks. He felt strongly about bringing Christianity to the natives.

But the people of Mactan and their leader, Lapulapu, didn't want to be Christians. They rejected Ferdinand's religion. In turn, he declared war on them.

A memorial statue of the Mactan leader, Lapulapu, stands on Mactan Island.

On April 27, 1521, the crew approached Mactan in rowboats. Lapulapu and his men waited on shore. They stood ready to fight. The natives far outnumbered Ferdinand and his men. Still, Ferdinand attacked. But he never got past the beach. He was killed in the battle.

*Mactans killed Ferdinand in a battle on April 27, 1521.*

Although their leader was dead, the men of Ferdinand's expedition continued their journey. They were still half a world away from their home in Spain. Only the *Victoria* finished the journey. On September 8, 1522, the remaining crew sailed the battered ship into Seville's harbor. Only eighteen men had survived. After nearly three years at sea, they had completed the first journey around the world.

Ferdinand's voyage did not open new trade routes as he had hoped. Sailing through the strait to the Pacific was too dangerous. But over time, people began to see how big the world is. They remembered Ferdinand's journey and understood his great accomplishment.

*277 men left Seville, Spain (LEFT), with Ferdinand in 1519. Only 18 men returned in 1522.*

Ferdinand showed that the world is twice as large as people had believed, and he proved once and for all that it is round. People remember Ferdinand for leading a voyage that changed maps forever. In the end, Ferdinand Magellan received the respect he had always wanted. He earned his place in history.

## MAGELLAN GOES TO VENUS

Ferdinand Magellan led the first journey around the world. In modern times, scientists named a spacecraft after him. But instead of traveling around Earth, the *Magellan* spacecraft orbited the planet Venus. From 1990 to 1994, *Magellan* circled the planet. The spacecraft mapped 98 percent of the planet's surface. Ferdinand would have been proud!

*While orbiting Earth, the Space Shuttle launches the MAGELLAN.*

# TIMELINE

## *In the year . . .*

1492   Ferdinand became a page in the service of Portugal's Queen Leonora.

1505   he joined Portugal's naval service.   Age 25

1513   he received a serious leg wound in battle. he returned to Portugal after eight years in the service.

1517   he gave up his Portuguese citizenship and went to Spain.

1518   he gained the support of the king of Spain, Charles I, to explore a westerly trade route to the Spice Islands.   Age 38

1519   Ferdinand's fleet sailed west to find the Spice Islands.

1520   his fleet arrived in Argentina. he discovered the passageway that would later be called the Strait of Magellan.

1521   he died in a battle with natives of the Philippines.   Age 41

1522   the remaining ship, *Victoria*, returned to Spain.

# DEAD RECKONING

Like many of today's maps, the maps Ferdinand Magellan studied before his journey had a grid of lines. Those that run east and west are called latitude lines. Those that run north and south are lines of longitude. These imaginary lines on the planet help pinpoint locations. In Ferdinand's time, sailors usually knew how far north or south they were. To find this out, they measured the distance from the horizon to the sun or to a nighttime star. This measurement helped them find their latitude.

But finding a ship's longitude was very difficult. There was no way to measure exactly how far east or west a ship was. Navigators used a compass and paid close attention to winds and currents. They made their best guesses to plot a ship's course. This type of navigation is called dead reckoning.

It was easy to make mistakes with dead reckoning. Ships often ended up hundreds of miles off course. Over time, many ships were lost and many sailors died because of poor guesswork. Ferdinand's focus on good navigation helped make his expedition a success.

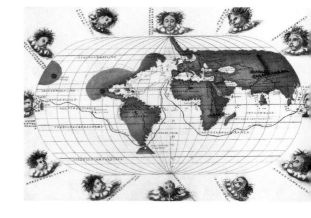

This 1540 world map shows lines of latitude and longitude.

# FURTHER READING

**Aller, Susan Bivin.** *Christopher Columbus.* **Minneapolis: Lerner Publications Company, 2003.** Learn about the life of the hero whose historic trip west to the Americas inspired Magellan.

**Fritz, Jean.** *Around the World in a Hundred Years: From Henry the Navigator to Magellan.* **New York: Putnam's, 1998.** Read how European exploration during the 1500s led to more accurate maps.

**Kramer, Sydelle.** *Who Was Ferdinand Magellan?* **New York: Grosset & Dunlap, 2004.** Explore the life of Ferdinand Magellan and his famous voyage around the world.

**MacGregor, Cynthia.** *Kids during the Age of Exploration.* **New York: PowerKids Press, 1999.** Find out how an apprentice to a mapmaker lived in Spain during the 1500s.

**Parker, Nancy Winslow.** *Land Ho! Fifty Glorious Years in the Age of Exploration.* **New York: HarperCollins, 2001.** Follow the adventures of Ferdinand Magellan and eleven other explorers who sailed to the Americas.

**Sansevere-Dreher, Diane.** *Explorers Who Got Lost.* **New York: TOR, 1992.** Learn about eight heroic explorers whose discoveries changed the map and changed the world.

**Watson, Charlie.** *Explorers: Atlas in the Round.* **Philadelphia: Running Press, 2001.** Discover history's greatest explorers, and trace their routes of discovery on detailed maps.

# WEBSITES

**Ferdinand Magellan**
**http://library.thinkquest.org/4034/magellan.html** Read
about the life of Ferdinand Magellan, and check out a
timeline of explorers.

**Magellan's Voyage around the World**
**http://www.socialstudiesforkids.com/subjects/**
**magellan.htm** Find a brief biography of Ferdinand
Magellan, and learn about the story of his voyage around
the world.

**The Mariners' Museum: Age of Exploration**
**http://www.mariner.org//educationalad/ageofex/** Through
biographies, a timeline, and activities, learn about the
explorers who sailed the world's seas.

# SELECT BIBLIOGRAPHY

Benson, E. F. *Ferdinand Magellan.* New York: Harper &
Brothers, 1930.

Bergreen, Laurence. *Over the Edge of the World:
Magellan's Terrifying Circumnavigation of the Globe.*
New York: William Morrow, 2003.

Daniel, Hawthorne. *Ferdinand Magellan.* New York:
Doubleday, 1964.

Joyner, Tim. *Magellan.* New York: McGraw-Hill, 1994.

Pigafetta, Antonio. *The First Voyage around the World
(1519–1522): An Account of Magellan's Expedition.*
Translated by Theodore J. Cachey. New York: Marsilio
Publishers, 1995.

# INDEX

Almeida, Francisco de, 14

Canary Islands, 22
Charles I (king of Spain), 18
Christianity, 8, 22, 39
Columbus, Christopher, 8, 9, 22

dangers at sea, 23, 24, 27, 29, 31, 33, 35, 36

Haro, Cristóbal de, 19
Humabon, (Cebu leader), 39, 40

India House, 11
Isle of Thieves (Guam), 37

John II (king of Portugal), 7, 10

Lapulapu (Mactan leader), 40
Leonora (queen of Portugal), 7

*Magellan,* 43
Magellan, Ferdinand: birth and childhood, 6–10; death, 41; employment, 7, 11, 12–13, 14

Manuel I (king of Portugal), 12, 15
Mar Pacífico (Pacific Ocean), 34
Molucca Islands (Spice Islands), 9, 15, 17, 18, 35

Philippines, 38–41; Cebu, 39, 40; Mactan, 40
Pigafetta, Antonio, 33
Port San Julian, Argentina, 29, 31

rebellions, 19, 23, 30
rules during the voyage, 22, 23

ships: *Concepción,* 20; *San Antonio,* 20, 34; *Santiago,* 20, 31; *Trinidad,* 20, 36; *Victoria,* 20, 24, 42
Strait of Magellan, 32–33

violence, 13, 14, 30, 37, 41

## Acknowledgments

**For photographs and artwork:** The images in this book are used with the permission of: © Stock Montage/SuperStock, p. 4; © The Granger Collection, New York, pp. 7, 17, 18, 29; Library of Congress, pp. 9 (S-P-HIST-EaAM-8697), 19 (S-P-ART-MAPS-8768); © Historical Picture Archive/CORBIS, p. 12; © Stapleton Collection/CORBIS, pp. 14, 30; © age fotostock/SuperStock, p. 22; © SuperStock, Inc./SuperStock, pp. 23, 24; © Independent Picture Service, p. 25; © Bridgeman Art Library, London/SuperStock, p. 27; © Lynn M. Stone, p. 28; © North Wind/North Wind Picture Archives, pp. 33, 39; © John Kruel/Independent Picture Service, p. 34–35; © Getty Images, pp. 36, 38, 41; © Michael S. Yamashita/CORBIS, p. 37; © Tony Arruza/CORBIS, p. 40; © Archivo Iconografico, S.A./CORBIS, p. 42; NASA/NSSDC, p. 43; © Huntington Library/SuperStock, p. 45. Front cover: Library of Congress (LC-USZ62-30424). Back cover: © The Granger Collection, New York.